# faith first

Legacy Edition

# Additional Activities

A Blackline Master Book
with Answer Key

## Grade Two

Rosanne Coury
Dee Ready

RCL✳
Benziger®

www.FaithFirst.com

**NIHIL OBSTAT**
Rev. Msgr. Robert M. Coerver
Censor Librorum

**IMPRIMATUR**
† Most Rev. Charles V. Grahmann
Bishop of Dallas

June 27, 2005

The Nihil Obstat and Imprimatur are official declarations that the material reviewed is free of doctrinal or moral error. No implication is contained therein that those granting the Nihil Obstat and Imprimatur agree with the contents, opinions, or statements expressed.

Acknowledgements

Scripture excerpts are based on the *New American Bible with Revised New Testament and Psalms* copyright © 1991, 1986, 1970, Confraternity of Christian Doctrine, Washington, DC. Used with permission. All rights reserved. No part of the *New American Bible* may be reproduced by any means without the permission of the copyright owner.

Send all inquiries to:
RCL • Resources for Christian Living
200 East Bethany Drive
Allen, Texas 75002-3804

Toll Free     877-275-4725
Fax             800-688-8356

Visit us at www.RCLweb.com
              www.FaithFirst.com

Printed in the United States of America

**20492**    ISBN 0-7829-1088-2

# Contents

# Introduction

One of the guiding principles of the *Faith First Legacy* program is that we want students to understand the faith of the Catholic Church and how to live out that faith in everyday life. The *Faith First Legacy Additional Activities* extend the faith knowledge of the children. The activities invite the students to think, reflect, and integrate the faith of the Church into their lives. They might do these activities alone, with groups in class, or at home. Versatility of use was a key element in writing and designing the activities. These engaging activities may be used anytime, anywhere—it's up to you.

Growing as a person of faith includes learning to look at one's actions and the world in a different way—in a faith-filled way. When we see things through the prism of faith, all is changed. The *Faith First Legacy Additional Activities* help to polish that prism, enriching the students and their world.

God bless you in your work, and have a great year!

# Find God's Goodness

Good things are signs of God's love for us.

Look carefully at the picture below.
Color all the signs of God's love you see.

# Draw Someone Taking Care of You

Jesus once said, "You are more important to God than the birds and all the animals. Trust him" (based on Matthew 6:26–34).

Draw a picture of someone taking care of you. Thank God for that person.

God takes care of me!

# Pray Our Belief in the Holy Trinity

The Sign of the Cross reminds us about the Holy Trinity. Practice praying the Sign of the Cross.

### The Sign of the Cross

We pray,

| | |
|---|---|
| **1** | In the name of the Father, |
| **2** | and of the Son, |
| **3** **4** | and of the Holy Spirit. |
| **5** | Amen. |

# Show Your Belief in the Holy Trinity

The children below believe in the Holy Trinity. Today they are at Mass. To show their belief in the Holy Trinity, they are making the Sign of the Cross. Draw yourself in the picture with the other children.

# Write a Creation Poem

Use the words below to write a poem.
Thank and praise God the Creator.
Then color the border. Make the border
as colorful as God's creation.

**ME**     **GOD**     **THANKS**

**PRAY**     **CREATION**

## My Creation Poem

I am as happy as can be!

God made the world and God

made _____.

_____ is what God has done
to make our world a lovely one.

For when I love and serve and _____,

I'm more and more like _____ each day.

So listen, Father, as I sing

My _____ to you for everything!

# Discover How God Shares Life with You

God is the Creator of everything that is good. He gives life to everyone.

Look at the Tree of Life. Find God's name at the roots of the tree. Then do the following to show God giving life:

1. Write your name on the trunk.

2. Write the names of some of your family members on the branches.

3. In the leaves, write something you enjoy in God's world.

4. Now thank God for the gift of your life.

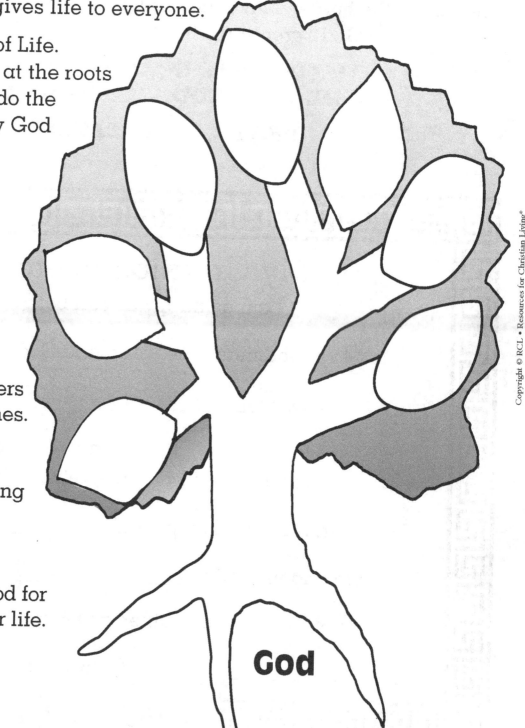

God

**Name** _____

# Sing to God

Here is a secret message. To discover it, circle the first letter in each group of letters. Then circle every other letter in each of the groups. Next, copy the letters you circle on the lines. Then read the message.

**PBSCADLEMFS**

_ _ _ _ _

**AHRIE**

_ _ _

**PKRLAMYNEORPS**

_ _ _ _ _ _

**PRESOTPULVE**

_ _ _ _ _

**SXIYNZG**

_ _ _ _

**TBO**

_ _

**GDOED!**

_ _ _

# Discover God's Wonderful World

Read Psalm 148 on page 39 in your textbook. Listen to all creation praising God.

Ask a grown-up to set up a mirror outdoors for you. Put it where you can see the beauty of God's creation in it. Now look in the mirror. See how different everything looks? In the picture of the mirror on this page, draw what you see.

**Name** _____

# Follow Jesus by Caring

People who follow Jesus care for others. Make a card to give to someone who needs your love today. Tell the person God cares for all people.

1. Fill out the inside of your card.

2. Color the pictures inside.

3. Cut out your card.

4. Fold your card in the middle.

5. Decorate the outside.

✂ INSIDE CARD

## My Caring Card

Dear _____,

God cares about you.
I care about you, too!
To show you that I care
I will

_____

Love,

_____

# Tell the Nativity Story

Everyone likes a good story. Many of us also like pictures to go with our stories. The story of Jesus' birth is called the Nativity story. Draw Mary and Joseph in the picture of the Nativity story. Be sure to include yourself in it too. Tell the Nativity story to your family.

# Get Ready for Jesus

Saint John the Baptist told people to get ready for Jesus. He said, "You have made bad choices. Make good ones now! Then you will be ready for Jesus" (based on Matthew 3:2–3).

God helps us make good choices. Good choices help us to get ready for Jesus.

Look at the pictures. Circle the pictures that show good choices. Put an X through the pictures that show bad choices.

# Make Good Choices

You want to hear Saint John the Baptist preach. But you must cross the Jordan River to get to him.

Use the stepping-stones in the picture to help you cross the river. But watch out. Some stones will not help you. Choose the stones that will help you reach Saint John the Baptist. Color those stones. Put an X on the stones that will not help you.

**Listen**

**Pray**

**Hit Someone**

**Disobey**

**Be Caring**

**Love God**

**Steal**

**Say, "I'm sorry."**

**Tell a Lie**

**Name** _____

# Make Sentences About Jesus

You are learning about Jesus.

Make five sentences that tell about Jesus.
Match the sentence beginnings in Column
A with the sentence endings in Column B.
Draw lines to connect the sentence
beginnings with their correct endings.
When you are finished, color the picture.

**Column A**

1. The name of God's Son is

2. God forgives us

3. Jesus always

4. Jesus died

5. God raised Jesus

**Column B**

loves everyone.

from the dead.

on the cross.

Jesus.

when we sin.

# Tell a Story About Jesus

Remember the Gospel tells us about Jesus' dying and rising? Put the four pictures about Jesus' dying and rising in the correct order. Use the pictures to tell others about Jesus.

1. Number what happened first with the number 1.

2. Number what happened second with the number 2 and what happened third with the number 3.

3. Number what happened last with the number 4.

4. Print the number for each picture in the empty box.

5. Color the pictures.

6. Tell the story of Jesus' dying and rising to a family member or a friend.

**Name** _____

# Make a Recipe for Friendship with Jesus

Soon you will join with other people and receive Jesus, the Bread of Life, in Holy Communion at Mass. This shows you are a special friend of Jesus. Until then, you can show you are a good friend of Jesus by doing good things.

Many people have favorite recipes. Read the recipe below for being a good friend. Then write one more thing to put in your recipe for being a friend of Jesus.

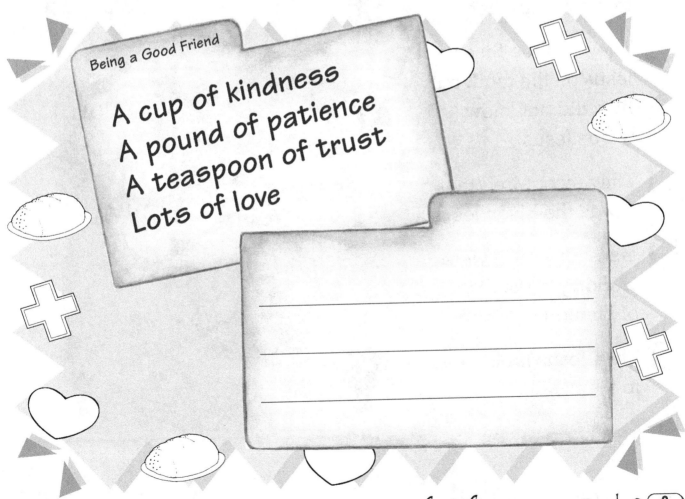

Being a Good Friend

A cup of kindness
A pound of patience
A teaspoon of trust
Lots of love

# Tell the Story of Emmaus

Some of Jesus' disciples were confused about Jesus' death and Resurrection. The Risen Jesus helped them to understand.

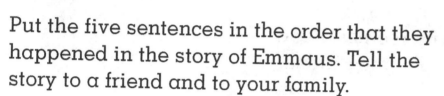

Put the five sentences in the order that they happened in the story of Emmaus. Tell the story to a friend and to your family.

☐ They asked Jesus to stay and eat with them.

☐ They met the Risen Jesus on the road, but they did not know it was Jesus.

☐ They recognized that it was the Risen Jesus!

☐ Jesus' disciples were walking to the town of Emmaus.

☐ Then Jesus broke the bread and gave it to them.

# Celebrate the Birthday of the Church

On Pentecost, the Holy Spirit came to Jesus' disciples. They taught and baptized many people that day. Pentecost is sometimes called the birthday of the Church.

Decorate this birthday cake for the Church.

Now you are ready to celebrate. Thank God for giving us the Church.

# Color the Children of God

The Holy Spirit helps us to live as children of God. Draw your face and other faces of God's children. Ask the Holy Spirit to teach you and help you live as a child of God.

**Chapter 9** The Holy Spirit

# Honor Mary

We honor Mary as the Mother of the Church. We honor Mary when we choose to live as her Son, Jesus, taught us to live. Decide on something you will do to honor Mary. Then draw a picture of yourself doing it.

# Invite People to Follow Jesus

Jesus told his first followers, "Invite all people to follow me" (based on Matthew 28:19). Jesus asks us to invite people to follow him too. Who would you invite?

1. Print the names of some people you want to come to know about Jesus.

2. Write their names on the guest list. Then add color to your guest list.

3. Each week, tell one person on the list about Jesus.

# Grow Strong as a Child of God

Eating good food helps make you healthy. Worshiping God together helps us become healthier children of God. Look at the bowl of alphabet soup below. Find and color these three words that help us grow as children of God.

**PRAISE     SACRAMENTS     WORSHIP**

# Share Your Feelings About a Miracle

Reread the Gospel story of Jesus healing the daughter of Jairus. Then color the four pictures.

Now flip a coin onto the page. Which picture did your coin land on or closest to? Pretend you are the person in the picture. Describe your feelings when Jairus's daughter got better. Share your feelings with your classmates.

Jesus and the disciples

Jairus

Jairus' daughter

Jairus' friends

# Interview Someone About Your Baptism

Baptism is a wonderfully special event. We become a member of our Church family.

Interview someone who was at your Baptism. Ask the person the questions below. On a piece of paper write what the person tells you.

The name of the person who I interviewed is

_____.

My Questions

1. When was I baptized?

2. Where was I baptized?

3. Who were my godparents?

4. Who else was at my Baptism?

5. What else do you remember about my Baptism?

# Draw Your Baptism

We celebrate Baptism with words and actions. Draw a picture of your Baptism. Include the people, church decorations, and other things that were part of your Baptism celebration.

## Seek Forgiveness and Peace

Forgiveness brings peace. We all need forgiveness sometimes. We need to forgive people too. The "Peace Pass" will help you make peace with someone whom you have hurt.

Fill in and color your "Peace Pass." Color the pictures and the words. Give your pass to the person you have hurt.

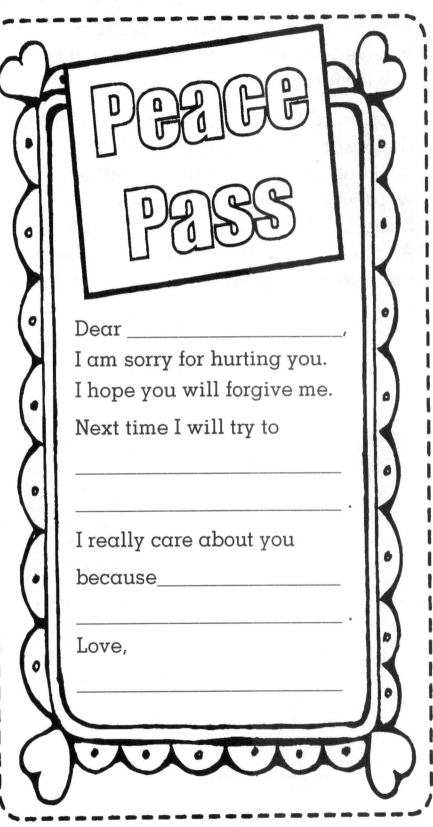

Peace Pass

Dear _____,
I am sorry for hurting you.
I hope you will forgive me.
Next time I will try to

_____
_____.

I really care about you

because_____

_____.

Love,

_____

# Play Forgiveness Charades

We use words and actions to show forgiveness. We use words and actions to ask for forgiveness too.

Each word below describes a feeling from the parable of the Forgiving Father. Without saying the word, act out each word with a partner for the whole class. See if they can guess your feeling word. Afterward, talk about how these words are part of forgiveness.

### Feeling Words

LONELY

SORROWFUL

HAPPY

REJOICING

PEACEFUL

**Name** _____

# Learn About a Special Forgiveness Place

The Catholic Church has a special place for people to confess their sins. We call this place the confessional. Sometimes we call it a reconciliation room.

Go to your parish church and find this special place. Take someone special with you. Look around. What did you see?

In the space below, write or draw what you saw.

# Use a Code to Find Forgiveness Words

There are four actions that are part of every celebration of the sacrament of Reconciliation. Your teacher has left you a picture code. It is a list of the four actions in Reconciliation. Use the key below to discover the four actions. Tell a friend and your family about each of the actions.

**Key**

A = ♡     E = ☮     I = ✚

O = ☆     U = 🕊

C☆NF☮SS✚☆N

_____

C☆NTR✚T✚☆N

_____

P☮N♡NC☮

_____

♡BS☆L🕊T✚☆N

_____

**Name** _____

# Sing Your Good News

Read the celebration song below. If you want, make up a melody and sing it. Then follow the directions. Celebrate your faith.

Take out your box of crayons or markers.

1. Put a BLUE CIRCLE around the words **listen, pray, speaks, hear, share, sing,** and **feel.**

2. Put a GREEN BOX around **Good news.**

3. Put a RED HEART around **Jesus, Lord,** and **me.**

4. Color the border.

**MY CELEBRATION SONG!**

Oh, listen carefully and pray,
For Jesus speaks good news today.
And when I hear the Gospel's word,
It's Jesus that I know I've heard.

Good news is what he has to share
With all God's People, everywhere.
With happy thanks, we sing and pray.
We gather in our church today.

Each day our Lord will bring good news.
His good news makes each person sing.
And I feel special and carefree
Because he loves to talk to me!

# Color Special Mass Clothes

Priests and deacons wear special clothes at Mass.

We call these special clothes vestments.

Color this vestment that the priest wears at Mass. Choose green, purple, or gold.

# Sing a Mass Song

Christians have always sung songs to God.

Here is a special Mass song for you to sing.

Sing the words to the tune for "Kum Ba Ya."
Ask your parents or teacher to sing it
with you. After you have sung the song,
color the children from various lands.

## My Mass Song

At this table, Lord,
We are one,

Brought together, Lord,
by your Son.

In this Bread and Wine,
Jesus come!

O Lord, Jesus, come!

Name _____

# Solve a Last Supper Puzzle

Jesus celebrated the Last Supper with his disciples. At the Eucharist the Church does what Jesus did at the Last Supper. Solve this puzzle.

## Across

1. We gather at _____ to share Jesus' Body and Blood.

5. The Jewish people celebrate their freedom in the _____ feast.

6. We gather round the _____ to celebrate the Eucharist.

## Down

2. The Last _____ was shared by Jesus and his disciples in Jerusalem.

3. At the Last Supper, Jesus gave thanks to _____.

4. Jesus blessed _____ and wine.

**Chapter 16** The Last Supper: A Scripture Story

# Give Thanks to God

At Mass the Church gives thanks to God.
What do you want to give thanks to God for?

When you ride in a car, you often see
billboards. Billboards tell us many things.
Create your own colorful billboard. Put a
thank you message to God on it. Show it to
your family.

# Write About Being Thankful

Jesus gave thanks to God the Father. At the
end of Mass we say "Thanks be to God."
Write an e-mail about being thankful.
Share your e-mail with a friend.

**Be Thankful**

# Grow with Good Choices

We grow as God's children when we make good choices. We make good choices when we follow Jesus.

Follow the footprints to Jesus. Color the footstep with words that name good choices. But watch out! Be sure to choose the footprints that lead to Jesus. When you finish, draw yourself in the picture with Jesus.

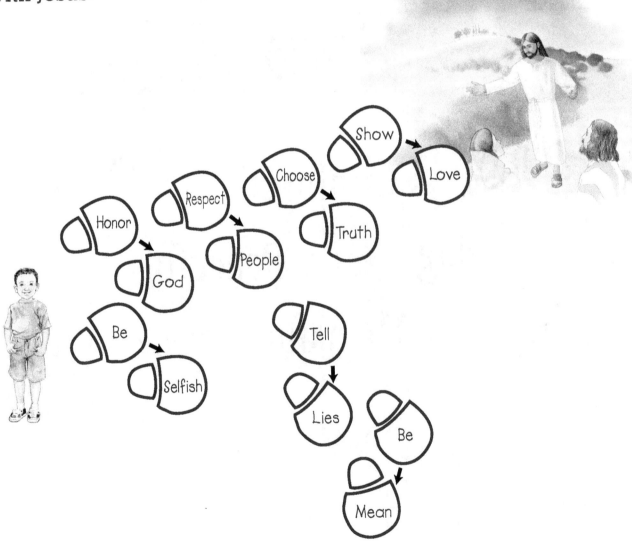

# Discover a Holy Spirit Symbol

The Holy Spirit helps us make good choices
to live as children of God. How do you feel
about yourself when you make choices to
love God and other people as Jesus taught?
Circle the words that tell how you feel.
Then connect the dots to find a symbol of
the Holy Spirit.

Happy

Angry     Confused     Proud

Loving     Peaceful

Thankful

Sad

# Make a Great Commandment Chain

Jesus told us to live the Great Commandment. He said to love God, ourselves, and our neighbors. Here is a way to remember what Jesus told us.

Follow the directions. Make a Great Commandment chain. It will help you remember to keep the Great Commandment.

1. Color and cut out the hearts.

2. Paste together the number 1 hearts; paste together the number 2 hearts; paste together the number 3 hearts.

3. Punch a hole at the top of each pasted heart.

4. Loop a piece of yarn through the holes in your three pasted hearts.

5. Wear your chain around your neck. It will remind you to keep the Great Commandment.

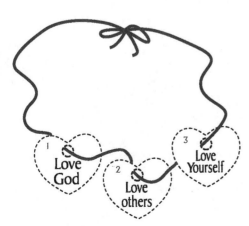

# Tell Others About the Great Commandment

The Great Commandment has two parts. The first part teaches that God is the center of our lives. The second part teaches us to respect and honor all people. Tell others about the Great Commandment. Create a web page for people around the world to see.

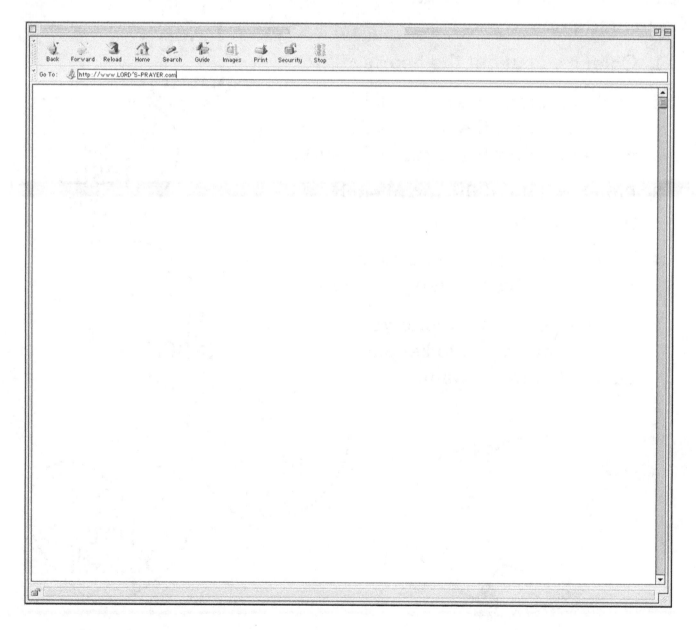

# Keep God's Laws

Jesus' followers keep the Ten Commandments. The Ten Commandments are God's laws. They are a gift from God to us. They are our treasure.

Color the treasure chest. Then find the poem about you and God. Write a title for the poem on the lid.

God's laws are a treasure
I keep within my heart.

God says I am a treasure he
keeps within his heart.

# Live by God's Laws of Love

The Ten Commandments are laws of love. They help us live a holy life.

Read each Commandment. Color the pictures next to each Commandment. Cut around the outer border and fold down the center. Keep the Commandments in your pocket. Or leave them in a place where you will see them every day when you get up.

Fold

Cut Here →

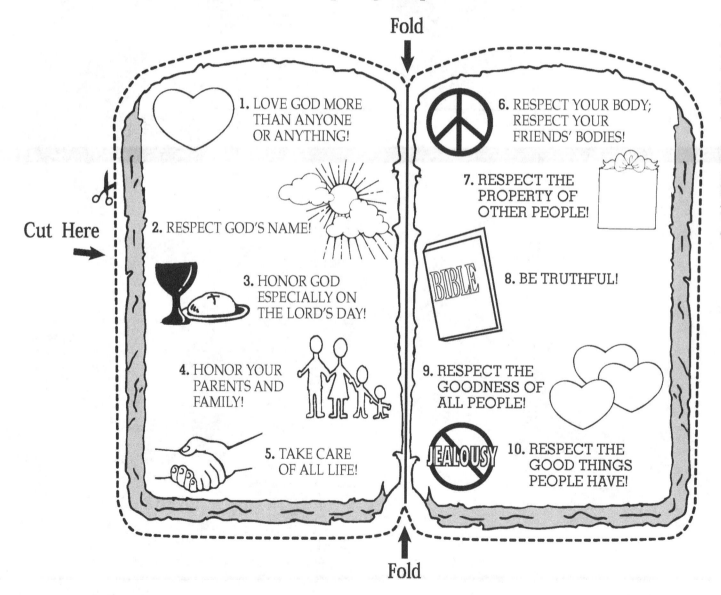

1. LOVE GOD MORE THAN ANYONE OR ANYTHING!

2. RESPECT GOD'S NAME!

3. HONOR GOD ESPECIALLY ON THE LORD'S DAY!

4. HONOR YOUR PARENTS AND FAMILY!

5. TAKE CARE OF ALL LIFE!

6. RESPECT YOUR BODY; RESPECT YOUR FRIENDS' BODIES!

7. RESPECT THE PROPERTY OF OTHER PEOPLE!

8. BE TRUTHFUL!

9. RESPECT THE GOODNESS OF ALL PEOPLE!

10. RESPECT THE GOOD THINGS PEOPLE HAVE!

Fold

# Create a Special Door

Sometimes you need help to make choices to live as followers of Jesus. You can always ask God to help you. Asking for God's help opens the door to good decisions.

The Book of Proverbs helps us to make wise choices. Let's make a reminder of what the Book of Proverbs teaches.

Read the words on the welcome mat. Then decorate the door. When you are finished, cut it out. Save your door to make the cover of a book for your next activity.

**Open the door to God's help.**

# Make a Book of Proverbs

God's proverbs in the Bible will help you make choices to live as a child of God. Make a special Proverb Book.

*Directions*

1. Fold a sheet of construction paper in half.

2. Read the proverbs tablets.

3. Decorate and color them.

4. Cut out the tablets and glue each tablet inside your book.

5. Glue the door you made in the last activity to the front cover of your Proverb Book.

6. Read your Proverb Book every day.

Trust God with all your heart.

Based on Proverbs 3:5

Speak kindly, and you will make peace.

Based on Proverbs 15:1

# Pray to Make Wise Choices

A wise choice is a choice that helps us live
as children of God. God the Father sent
Jesus to show us how to make wise choices.
We can ask God to help us make wise
choices.

Write a prayer.
Ask God to help
you make wise
choices. Ask
God to help you
follow Jesus.
Color the
pictures of the
children making
wise choices.
Pray your
prayer
whenever you
need help. Pray
your prayer
often.

Dear God,

I need your help to make a
wise choice. Please help me

_____

_____

_____

Thank you, God!

Love,

_____

# Going in the Right Direction to Choose God's Love

God helps us in many ways to make wise choices.

Look at the signs. They tell some things you can do to choose God's love.

Write 1 next to the sign you find most helpful. Pick out the idea that is the next most helpful. Write 2 next to it.

Keep choosing signs and writing down numbers until you finish numbering the signs. When you are done, add a new idea of your own in the empty road sign.

Color the picture. Hang it near your bed to remind you to choose God's love.

# Remember That God Forgives

Jesus teaches us to make wise choices.
Sometimes we do not make wise choices.
Then we need forgiveness.

What do we need to do to be forgiven? Solve the code to find out.

*Directions*

1. Cross out all the Qs, Xs, Js, and Zs.

2. Make words out of the letters that are left.

3. Write the words on the lines under the letters.

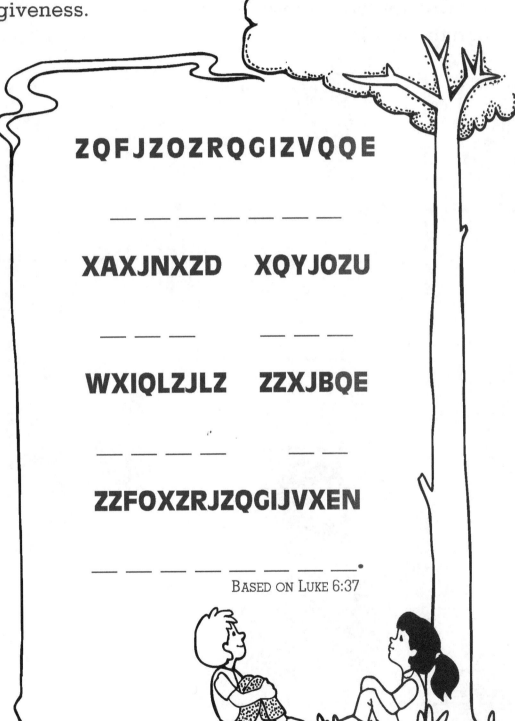

**ZQFJZOZRQGIZVQQE**

_ _ _ _ _ _ _

**XAXJNXZD**     **XQYJOZU**

_ _ _       _ _ _ _

**WXIQLZJLZ**     **ZZXJBQE**

_ _ _ _ _       _ _ _

_ _ _ _ _ _ _ _ _ _ _ .

BASED ON LUKE 6:37

# Learn to Sign "I am sorry."

God forgives us when we are sorry. Learn to sign "I am sorry." Sign the words when you ask God for forgiveness. Teach a friend to sign the words.

I

am

sorry

# Pray Anytime, Anyplace

Prayer is talking and listening to God. We can pray anytime and anyplace.

Make a badge that says you are a person of prayer.

*Directions*

1. Write your name on the line.

2. Color your badge.

3. Cut out the two pieces.

4. Glue each piece to its own index card.

5. Cut out the two pieces of badges again.

6. Paste the front and back pieces together.

7. Ask your teacher to punch a hole in the top of your badge and help you put yarn through it.

8. Wear your badge.

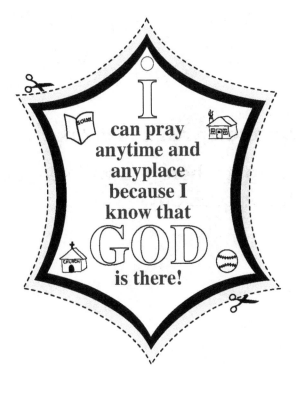

# Remember to Pray

We sometimes pray alone. We also pray with others. We praise God. We thank God. We ask God for help.

Make a bookmark that helps you to remember to pray.

*Directions*

1. Write a saying on your bookmark that will help you remember to pray every day.

2. Here are some words you can use:

| | |
|---|---|
| GOD | PRAISE |
| YOU | THANKS |
| ME | ASK |

3. Decorate your bookmark.

4. Keep it where you will see it many times each day.

# Pray the Our Father with Your Family

God is our Father. We are all children of God. We trust God. We pray to him as Jesus taught us to do. We pray the Our Father together.

Draw a picture of your family praying the Our Father together. Ask your family to pray the Our Father with you each day.

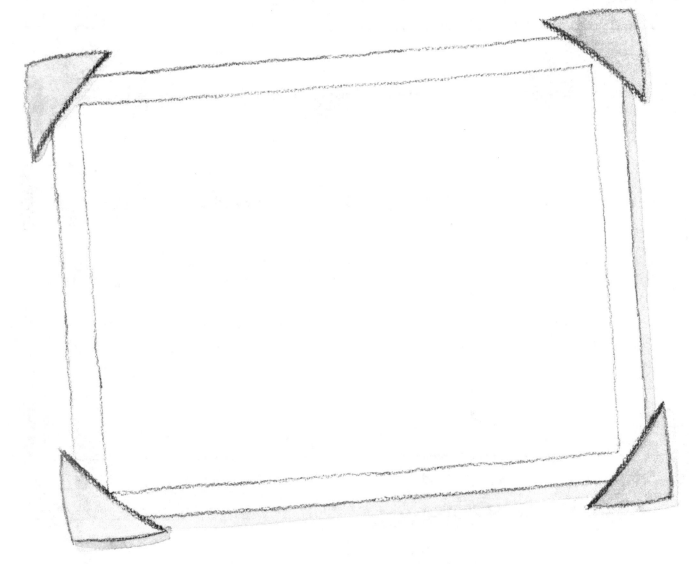

# Live the Our Father

Jesus taught us the Our Father. Use the code to find out what Jesus asks us to do.

*Directions*

1. Read and answer each question. If your answer is Yes, circle the letter under Yes. If your answer is No, circle the letter under No.

2. Write the letters you circled on the lines. Then you will know what Jesus asks you to do.

| | | YES | NO | | | YES | NO |
|---|---|---|---|---|---|---|---|
| **1.** | Is God our Father in Heaven? | G | O | **5.** | Do we ask God for our daily bread? | W | Q |
| **2.** | Is God's name holy? | O | M | **6.** | Do we forgive others? | I | Z |
| **3.** | Do we ask God's Kingdom to come? | D | S | **7.** | Do we ask God to lead us not into temptation? | L | T |
| **4.** | Does God want us to be good? | S | W | **8.** | Do we ask God to deliver us from evil? | L | P |

___  ___  ___  ___'  ___      ___  ___  ___  ___ !
  1    2    3    4        5    6    7    8

# Search for God's Kingdom

Jesus taught about God's kingdom. In the Our Father we pray "Thy kingdom come."

Discover the kingdom words in the puzzle.

| FATHER | FORGIVE |
|--------|---------|
| KINGDOM | NAME |
| BREAD | WILL |
| HEAVEN | |

1. Find the words from the box in the puzzle and circle them.

2. Color your picture.

3. Share your completed puzzle with your family. Begin by praying the Our Father.

```
N K I N G D O M P
B V O A P M B Y H
R M P M Q F X S F
E G U E K O L J A
A K T N G R O Z T
D J U Z L G J U H
N K P Q W I L L E
A U I F D V P M R
J H E A V E N M P
```

# Draw the Kingdom of God

The kingdom of God is also called the kingdom of heaven.

What do you think God's kingdom will be like? Draw a picture of it. Then show someone your picture.

# Wait for Jesus

During Advent we get ready for Jesus. We light the candles on the Advent wreath. We are extra kind to others.

Sing this song during Advent. It will help you get ready for Jesus. Sing it to the tune of "The Alphabet Song."

WE ARE WAITING FOR THE DAY

WHEN GOD'S SON COMES HERE TO STAY!

HEAL THE EARTH AND MAKE US ONE

IN THE NAME OF CHRIST THE SON!

SO WE SERVE AND TEACH TODAY.

"HURRY, LORD! COME SOON," WE PRAY.

# Make Jesus an Ornament

During the Christmas season, we remember that the Magi gave gifts to Jesus. We give gifts too. Read the poem below. It tells Jesus what your gift is.

Make your gift for Jesus into an ornament.

*Directions*

1. Decorate and color the two sides of the ornament.
2. Cut both sides out.
3. Paste them each on an index card.
4. Cut them both out again.
5. Paste the two sides together.
6. Punch a hole at the top and pull a piece of yarn through it.
7. Hang your ornament on your Christmas tree.
8. Tell Jesus how much you love him as you hang your ornament on the tree.

*My Gift to Jesus*

*Three Magi brought their treasures
To tiny Bethlehem.
They gave them all to Jesus.
He gave his love to them.*

*I have no gold or jewels.
No camels do I keep.
I have no frankincense or myrrh
To lay at Jesus' feet.*

*But oh! My heart is thankful
And filled with God's love too.
So that's my gift, Lord Jesus.
I give my heart to you!*

Name _____

## Make a Book to Help You Follow Jesus

During Lent we pray more often. We do more to help those in need. We try to love God more.

Make a flip book with this page. Your book will have ideas for 10 Lenten activities. Practice each idea four times during Lent. To make your book, do the following:

1. Draw a cross on an index card. Print your name on it.

2. Color the boxes. Then cut them out.

3. Glue each box to an index card.

4. Punch a hole in the top left-hand corner of each card.

5. Attach the cards by pulling yarn through each hole and tying it. Now your flip book is ready.

| |
|---|
| **PRAY FOR FIVE EXTRA MINUTES** |
| **TAKE TIME TO HELP A PARENT WITH A CHORE** |
| **FORGIVE SOMEONE WHO HURT YOU** |
| **READ A BIBLE STORY** |
| **WRITE A PRAYER OF THANKS** |
| **GIVE MONEY TO THE POOR** |
| **GIVE UP CANDY AND GUM** |
| **WRITE A NOTE TO SOMEONE WHO IS LONELY** |
| **DONATE FOOD TO THOSE IN NEED** |
| **GIVE UP ONE TV SHOW** |

# Serve as Jesus Taught

At the Last Supper Jesus taught us what serving others means. He served his disciples by washing their feet. He asked us to love and serve one another.

You have many opportunities to serve others. In the first box, draw how you will serve others at home. Then write what you will do.

In the second box, draw how you will serve others at school. Then write what you will do.

I will serve others at home by:

_____

_____

I will serve others at school by:

_____

_____

**Name** _____

# Find an Easter Egg Message

Easter is the BEST day! On Easter God raised Jesus to new life.

Some people have Easter egg hunts on Easter Sunday. Use the word or words on each egg in the basket to make an Easter message.

1. Jesus is __ __ __ __ __!

2. __ __ __ __ __ __ __ __ __ with Jesus!

3. We share __ __ __ __ __ __ __ __ in Jesus!

4. We belong __ __ __ __ __ __ __ __!

5. Easter is the __ __ __ __ __ __ __ __!

6. We are __ __ __ __ __ __ People!

# Grow Strong in the Holy Spirit

On Pentecost the Holy Spirit helped Peter talk to people. He asked them to make hard choices in their lives. Then they could follow Jesus.

All through Lent you also made hard choices. You became a stronger follower of Jesus. Write what you found hardest to do during Lent. Then explain how the Holy Spirit helped you to become a better follower of Jesus.

During Lent I found it hardest to _____

_____

_____

_____

The Holy Spirit helped me to be strong when _____

_____

_____

_____

# Answer Key

## CHAPTER 3

**Write a Creation Poem**

"My Creation Poem"

I am as happy as can be!

God made the world and God
  made ME.

CREATION is what God has done
  to make our world a lovely one.

For when I love and serve and PRAY,

I'm more and more like GOD each day.

So listen, Father, as I sing

My THANKS to you for everything!

## CHAPTER 4

**Sing to God**

Psalms are prayers people sing to God!

## CHAPTER 6

**Get Ready for Jesus**

Middle right and bottom right: good choices.
Upper right and left: bad choices.

**Make Good Choices**

The stones with the following words
should be colored: Listen; Pray; Be Caring;
Love God; Say, "I'm sorry".

## CHAPTER 7

**Make Sentences About Jesus**

1. The name of God's Son is Jesus.
2. God forgives us when we sin.
3. Jesus always loves everyone.
4. Jesus died on the cross.
5. God raised Jesus from the dead.

**Tell a Story About Jesus**

Clockwise: 3, 1, 4, 2

## CHAPTER 8

**Tell the Story of Emmaus**

1. Jesus' disciples were walking to the
   town of Emmaus.
2. They met the Risen Jesus on the road,
   but they did not know it was Jesus.
3. They asked Jesus to stay and eat
   with them.
4. Then Jesus broke the bread and gave
   it to them.
5. They recognized that it was the
   Risen Jesus!

## CHAPTER 11

**Grow Strong as a Child of God**

SACRAMENTS

WORSHIP

PRAISE

## CHAPTER 14

**Use a Code to Find Forgiveness Words**

CONFESSION

CONTRITION

PENANCE

ABSOLUTION

## CHAPTER 16

**Solve a Last Supper Puzzle**

Across:
1. Mass
5. Passover
6. Altar

Down:
2. Supper
3. God
4. Bread

# Answer Key

## CHAPTER 18

### Grow with Good Choices

The footprints that lead to Jesus say:

"Honor" / "God"
"Respect" / "People"
"Choose" / "Truth"
"Show" / "Love"

### Discover a Holy Spirit Symbol

The words that should be circled are:
Happy
Proud
Loving
Peaceful
Thankful

## CHAPTER 23

### Remember That God Forgives

Forgive and you will be forgiven.

## CHAPTER 25

### Live the Our Father

God's will!

## CHAPTER 26

### Search for God's Kingdom

## Triduum/Easter

### Find an Easter Egg Message

1. Jesus is risen!
2. We are one with Jesus!
3. We share new life in Jesus!
4. We belong to Jesus!
5. Easter is the best day!
6. We are Easter People!

CPSIA information can be obtained
at www.ICGtesting.com
Printed in the USA
LVHW060034020921
696627LV00005B/27